LEONARDO DA VINCI

First edition for the United States, Canada,
and the Philippines published 1994
by Barron's Educational Series, Inc.

Design David West Children's Book Design
Compiled and researched by Gillian Bainbridge BA Hons, ATC

Designed and produced by
Aladdin Books Ltd
28 Percy Street
London W1P 9FF

All inquiries should be addressed to:
Barron's Educational Series, Inc.
250 Wireless Boulevard
Hauppauge, NY 11788

International Standard Book No. 0-8120-1828-1

Library of Congress Catalog Card No. 93-2385

Library of Congress Cataloging-in Publication Data
Hart, Tony, 1925-
Leonardo da Vinci / by Tony Hart. – 1st U.S. ed.
p. cm. – (Famous children)
Summary: Focuses on the childhood of the noted artist Leonardo da Vinci.
ISBN 0-8120-1828-1
1. Da Vinci, Leonardo, 1452-1519–Childhood and youth–Juvenile literature.
2. Artists–Italy–Biography–Juvenile literature. [1. Da Vinci, Leonardo,
1452-1519–Childhood and youth. 2. Artists.] I. Title. II. Series.
N6923.L33H37   1993
709'.2–dc20   93-2385
[B]   CIP   AC

Special thanks to: The Royal Collection ©, Her Majesty Queen Elizabeth II; Bridgeman
Art Library; Giraudon/Bridgeman Art Library; British Museum, London; Roger Vlitos; Scala, Florence.
The publishers have made every effort to contact all the relevant copyright holders
and apologize for any omissions that may have inadvertently been made.
Printed in Belgium
34   98765432

Famous Children

LEONARDO DA VINCI

TONY HART
ILLUSTRATED BY SUSAN HELLARD

BARRON'S

On the day that Leonardo da Vinci was born, his proud grandfather, Antonio, wrote in his own grandfather's notebook, "Saturday, April 15th at 10:30 P.M. 1452, there was born to me a grandson, the child of Ser Piero, my son." Leonardo was born near Vinci in Italy. His family had taken the name of the town as their surname.

Leonardo's parents did not marry, so although he spent his first months being nursed by his mother, Caterina, Leonardo soon went to live with his father's parents, Antonio and Monna Lucia da Vinci.

"It is such a pleasure to have a young baby in the house again," sighed Monna Lucia happily.

Leonardo's father, Ser Piero, was a busy lawyer. He soon married and was often away. Caterina lived nearby and Leonardo could often visit her. She, too, married and had five more children.

Leonardo's uncle, Francesco, looked after the family estate, and Leonardo went everywhere with him, tending the olive trees and grapevines and learning a love of nature.

When Leonardo was only four years old, he watched with his uncle as a hurricane tore through the countryside, destroying everything in its path. It passed close by Vinci and could be clearly seen from there. Leonardo never forgot the experience and, as a man, he was fascinated by weather and the power of nature.

Leonardo was born with remarkable gifts. He was physically beautiful and full of charm. He was clever, too. His mind was always so busy that he would set himself many things to learn – only to move on to something else immediately.

Leonardo was forever scribbling in notebooks. He had a very strange way of writing. He wrote with his left hand in reverse. The only way to read it easily was to look at it in a mirror!

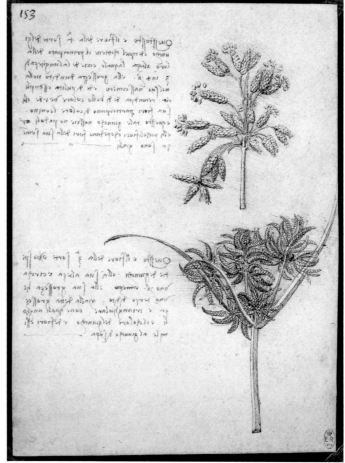

Leonardo had only a limited education in Vinci but his great talents were obvious to his teachers.

"I cannot teach you any more about mathematics, Leonardo," said his baffled teacher. "I have taught you all I know."

Leonardo attended music lessons and learned to play the lyre. He was soon writing his own songs.

"I have never heard such good verse and lovely singing," said his music teacher.

Leonardo not only wrote in his notebooks. From an early age, he did wonderful drawings to record his thoughts and observations as he roamed the beautiful Italian countryside.

Eventually even Ser Piero realized that Leonardo's drawing ability was special. He took some of Leonardo's work to show his close friend, Andrea del Verrocchio, who ran a very successful artists' workshop in Florence.

"Shall I allow Leonardo to study design?" asked Ser Piero.

Verrocchio was amazed by the drawings and urged Piero to bring his son to the workshop. Leonardo was delighted to hear the news.

"Florence will seem very big and strange after living in a village," he said, "but I can't wait to see it and to learn so many new things."

So, at twelve years old, Leonardo joined his father in a house overlooking the government offices of Florence where Ser Piero worked.

At Verrocchio's, Leonardo began by running errands and sweeping the floor. But soon he was making brushes, stretching canvases, and preparing paints.

Everyone at the workshop learned to draw from nature. Leonardo soon attracted his master's attention.

He made clay models and draped the figures with cloth dipped in plaster, which then hardened.

"Now I can draw the folds as they really are," he explained.

"What a good idea," said Verrocchio. "We must all learn to look and to see."

If Leonardo saw a face he wanted to draw, he would follow the person around all day long until he could remember that face exactly. Then he would rush home to make his drawing as if the person were still there.

"An artist must be like a mirror," he would say, "reflecting what is placed right in front of it."

Leonardo loved being at the workshop, and found Florence an exciting place to live.

In the winter of 1466, a flood surged through Florence in the middle of the night. Houses and churches were engulfed. Horses were drowned in their stables. It was soon over but the devastation was dreadful to see. Once again, Leonardo was reminded of the power of nature's forces.

At this time, too, Florence suffered another bout of the plague. Its ruler, Lorenzo de Medici, decided it was time to cheer everyone up and arranged lots of parties and festivities. Verrocchio's studio had to help with the many banners and costumes.

"Can you design a helmet for the Duke of Milan?" Verrocchio asked Leonardo.

Leonardo produced a wonderful design.

One day Ser Piero was at his country home in Vinci, when one of the peasants on the farm asked him a favor.

"I have made a shield out of a fig tree I have cut down. Could you get someone to paint it for me when you return to Florence?"

He promised to pay in fish and game, so Ser Piero was happy to agree.

When Leonardo saw the shield, he said, "I cannot paint on that. I shall have to reshape and polish it first."

He transformed the shield into a beautiful object. Then he thought carefully about the design he would paint on it.

"I know! I shall invent my own creature," said Leonardo. "I shall make studies of live lizards, snakes, and bats and put them together to make a terrifying monster."

When Ser Piero saw the shield, he jumped with horror. He thought it was a real monster.

"Good!" said Leonardo. "The shield has produced the right reaction. Now you can take it away."

Verrocchio asked for Leonardo's help with a large painting for the monastery at San Salvi.

Leonardo was allowed to paint the angel carrying Christ's garment. Leonardo was still very young, but his painting was excellent.

"Your painting is beautiful, Leonardo. It is even better than mine. I shall never use colors again," vowed Verrocchio.

To the delight of Leonardo and Ser Piero, he made Leonardo his partner.

Leonardo loved animals, and when he was twenty he became a vegetarian. He would buy caged birds just so he could set them free. He would study and draw birds in flight.

"I wish I could fly," he thought, and so he designed a flying machine with flapping wings and a "helicopter."

Leonardo invented a bicycle 300 years before the first one was built!

He wrote to the Duke of Milan,

"Most illustrious Lord, I have invented thirty-six secret ways of helping you with your military engineering . . ."

One of them was a tank!

Leonardo's talents and achievements were so many and so great that people could hardly believe he was mortal.

Leonardo died in the arms of the King of France when he was seventy-five years old. Today his Mona Lisa is the most precious painting in the world.